FLASH...
THE
MOST
AVAILABLE
LIGHT

The fastest, easiest way to maximize the potential of your hand held flash
when shooting DIGITAL and FILM

Quest C. Couch III

Fallenwater Publishing
New Braunfels, TX

First edition 2004
Published by Fallenwater Publishing
28540 Durango Dr., New Braunfels, TX 78132 - USA

Publisher: Heidi Kenny
Production Editors: Leslie Staas
                           Roberta Skeckowski
Cover Design: Roger Christian
Layout and Design: Paula McCoy
Illustrations: Laura A. Hotten
Image Processing: Paul Vaughn

Information provided in this book is correct to the best of the publisher's knowledge; all other liability is expressly disclaimed. Due to specification changes by manufacturers without notice, the contents of the book may not necessarily agree with changes made after publication.

Printed in China

Is This The Book For You?

• Are you considering a detachable flash for your digital or film camera but are concerned about the equipment and results?

• Are you currently confused and dissatisfied with the results of your flash photography?

• Are you interested in maximizing the potential of your flash?

• Do you wish to avoid the "flashed" look and create more natural images?

• Do you want the process to be simple, fast and fun?

If you answered yes to any of these questions, then this is your book…read on.

Flash...The MOST available light

INTRODUCTION

For both professionals and serious amateurs, flash is playing an increasingly important and creative role in imaging. The sophistication of today's camera/flash systems enables the photographer to do more, faster, with greater consistency.

This book is the result of several decades of flash photography, accessory design **(Etc. # 7)** and thousands of conversations with both novice and experienced photographers. Many of the techniques we will be discussing were, of course, originally developed using traditional film cameras but are equally applicable to Digital Imaging **(Etc. #1)**. We invite you to draw on this experience and discover that flash really is the MOST available light.

If you have further questions, visit **www.lumiquest.com**, "Ask Quest" and we will make every effort to provide prompt, accurate answers.

Good Shooting

Quest C. Couch III

How to use this book

This book is designed to be a "quick read," initially providing an easy to understand working overview to the reader. More in-depth explanations are offered in the "Etc." section; in fact, 70% of the book is composed of the "Etc." section. These can be either read the first time through or referred back to as the need arises.

This book is not intended to replace your flash instruction manual; on the contrary, an understanding of the operation of your flash is very important. You might, however, find it valuable to read this book prior to your instruction manual since that manual was probably written by engineers and this book was written by a photographer. You might even want to read this book prior to selecting a flash since it could help you make a better buying decision. We will not review in detail particular models of flash units or other equipment; rather, we will provide a broader perspective applicable to all quality equipment. Each manufacturer and model will have somewhat different ways of accomplishing the same task. Our objective is to help you understand when and why you should use features to accomplish your objectives.

Your flash is one of the most powerful and creative tools in your camera bag. This book will allow you to realize the potential of that tool.

INDEX

FLASH...THE **MOST** AVAILABLE LIGHT

Chapter 1: So...Why Does Flash Photography Often Look so Unnatural?

The available light that illuminates a scene is generally accepted as "natural" if it was not introduced solely for the purpose of photographing that scene. It might be direct or diffused sunlight, a street lamp, a sign or any other light source inherent to the scene. A sunrise in the Rockies and neon signs on the strip in Las Vegas are both accepted as "natural" available light because they are characteristic of their respective environments.

Flash photography often looks very unnatural because it introduces a light source for photographic purposes which is clearly inconsistent with the natural lighting characteristics of the scene itself.

In order to overcome this problem, we must address the three primary reasons why typical flash illumination appears unnatural. These reasons are not unique to flash photography but are inherently more acute and problematic when using a flash.

Direction

There are few places in nature where the observer is also the light source. No wonder our "on camera" flash shots tend to make your subject look like a deer caught in headlights.

Size

Few light sources in nature, none of them flattering, are as small and intense as the photographic flash and, as you will see, the size of the light source has a dramatic effect on light quality no matter what the source.

Uneven Illumination

Certainly there are dramatic lighting situations in nature, but when uneven illumination within a scene is caused by something clearly inconsistent with the scene itself (such as a photographic flash)...our brain reads... "HARSH...FAKE...FLASH...YUCK!"

So, what can we do about these problems? Well, a number of things…things that are quick, easy and just make common sense.

DIRECTION

Determine what would be a logical source of light for the scene you are photographing and either use that light source or give the illusion of that light source with your flash. This can be accomplished by either reflecting or bouncing **(Etc. # 2)** the light off some nearby surface that becomes the new light source or actually removing the flash from the camera or some combination of the two. In some cases you can use available light as the primary light source and your flash to "fill-in" harsh shadows or illuminate areas not affected by the available light. The key here is that the light sources are coming from a believable and natural (at least natural for that scene) direction **(Etc. # 5).**

SIZE

All other factors constant, the larger the light source, the softer the shadows **(Etc. # 4)**. The surface off which you bounce the light becomes the new (and larger) source of light. Or you can allow the light to refract through translucent diffusing material **(Etc. # 3)**. An illuminated piece of diffusion material on the front of a softbox that is many times larger than the flash head itself can make a dramatic improvement over the quality of light.

UNEVEN ILLUMINATION

Larger light sources generally provide more even illumination from left to right and top to bottom. However, the discrepancy between foreground and background illumination is not impacted by the size of the light source whatsoever **(Etc. # 6)**. This discrepancy is particularly problematic when using a flash due to the fact that distance from the flash to various objects in the frame may vary considerably. All other factors constant…objects closer to the light source than the correctly exposed subject will be overexposed; objects further from the light source than the correctly exposed subject will be underexposed. This discrepancy can be mitigated by moving the light source farther away from the subject, rearranging the subject, or using multiple flash units.

If you understand how these three issues impact your flash photography, learn the techniques to control them, and combine them with available light...you can eliminate unpleasant surprises and avoid that dreaded "flashed" look.

Your photographic flash is an incredibly versatile tool and, nestled in your camera bag, it is actually much more "available" than available light. The range of its uses in capable hands is nothing short of amazing...

- It can be your only source of light.
- It can be your primary source of light.
- It can be a secondary source of light.
- It can be as subtle as a catch light to make the eyes sparkle.
- It can reduce contrast in high contrast situations.
- It can increase contrast and add highlights in flat lighting situations.
- It can enhance textural variations in subjects of similar color.
- It can warm up cool, flat scenes.
- It can "stop" action and imply motion.

A fair question at this point would be "**How in the world can a flash accomplish ALL that?**" Well, it is almost entirely a function of how flash and existing available light interact and in what balance. It is actually pretty simple but it is easy to get bogged down in the technical terminology characteristic of manufacturer's instruction manuals.

THE RELATIONSHIP BETWEEN FLASH AND AVAILABLE LIGHT

In some situations your flash is not the only or even primary source of light; it can, however, be used in a variety of ways to enhance the image you are creating. To seamlessly blend flash and available light is one of the great joys of working with your flash...it can become a wonderful creative tool rather than simply a necessary evil. But, regardless of the role that you assign your flash in making an image, direction, size and evenness of illumination should still be taken into consideration.

Combining flash with available light is a major key to maximizing its potential. Its mastery is an indispensable photographic skill. It is important that you read the following and understand it completely before moving on because it will make the rest of this book make sense. Put aside for a minute the terminology used in your flash instruction manuals. Once you understand the concepts, objectives and techniques, the specific terminology used in the instruction manual for your particular flash will be much less confusing **(Etc. # 8)**. To exercise control over the process of combining flash and available light, you must understand what effects each individually and both combined.

Available light exposure is controlled by a combination of **aperture** and **shutter speed (Etc. # 9).**

Flash exposure is controlled by a combination of **aperture** and flash **power setting (Etc. # 9).**

As long as you stay with a shutter speed at least as slow as flash sync **(Etc. # 10)**, changing the shutter speed impacts the available light exposure but **not** the flash exposure.

Aperture changes impact overall exposure, **both** flash and available light.

So, given a **constant aperture**…

• If you change shutter speed it **only** impacts the portion of the image illuminated by available light.
• If you change flash power setting it **only** impacts the portion of the image illuminated by the flash.

And once again, if you change aperture it impacts both the portions of the scene illuminated by available light and flash.

It should be apparent by now that you have control over not only the overall exposure but also the relative impact of available light and flash in your image. You can choose balanced, flash dominant, or available light dominate and the degree to which one is dominant.

Here's how that happens …
Let's say you meter the available light and determine that correct exposure at f/8 can be obtained at a shutter speed of 1/60th. Personally,

I usually prefer my fill flash approximately 1 stop under available light exposure. I consider this my "balanced" fill flash. To accomplish this, you select a power setting for your flash to deliver correct flash exposure at f/5.6. At these settings, both available light and flash have a significant impact on overall exposure **(Photograph 1-A).**

OR: If you would like the area illuminated by available light to be **2 stops darker** than the area illuminated by flash, you set the shutter speed to 1/250th (sync speed). Flash exposure

Photograph 1-B: Flash Dominant

Photograph 1-A: Balanced

Photograph 1-C: Available Light Dominant

will **not** be effected but **available light** will be **2 stops darker** than flash exposure **(Photograph 1-B).**

OR: If you would like the area illuminated by **flash** to be **3 stops darker** than the area illuminated by available light, you leave the shutter speed at 1/60th and reduce flash power to -3. Then the flash will have minimal, if any, impact on the subject **(Photograph 1-C).**

These are only three alternatives, the possible ratios are endless.

It is up to **YOU** to determine the relative impact of various light sources on your image.

Some might call this available light photography with "fill flash."

Some might call this flash photography with "slow sync" to record available light.

Call it whatever you want…it is all a matter of blending light sources to your satisfaction to create the image you want. This balancing of light sources can be accomplished manually, with automatic flashes, and even easier using the controls available on typical dedicated camera/flash combinations **(Etc. # 9).**

If you evenly illuminate a scene with an appropriate balance of flash and available light coming from a natural direction, casting softer shadows from an enlarged light source, you are well on your way towards maximizing the potential of your flash.

It is said that "Photography is the Art of Painting with Light". Well, think of your flash as everything from a spray gun to a 9" roller to a pinpoint detail brush. It is up to you.

Allow yourself to become a student of light. Understand and appreciate the characteristics of natural, appropriate lighting…in a bedroom or kitchen, a church, a bar, a hospital, a factory or in a restaurant…all so different…each with a personality of its own **(Etc. # 11).**

CHAPTER II: MANAGING "TRADE-OFFS"

With the sophistication of today's camera/flash combinations, it is entirely possible to create technically perfect photographs relying solely on the automation of the camera and flash with little understanding of what is happening. In fact, all of the various flash/available light ratios discussed in the preceding chapter can be accomplished automatically. The severe limitation here is that the camera is not the least bit creative. Its sophisticated features are almost entirely automated versions of what creative, experienced professionals have been doing for years and, as mentioned before, the terms used to describe these features can be quite intimidating **(Etc. # 8)**. So, in order to maximize the potential of the equipment and add your eye and creativity into the equation, a basic understanding of what is happening technically is invaluable. And here is the great part...armed with this technical understanding, you can select the appropriate mode so that the camera/lens/flash combination does the things you want...AUTOMATICALLY. What must be avoided is allowing your equipment to make decisions without your knowledge. Remember, it is not the least bit creative. The degree to which some of the detailed technical information is of importance and interest to you will vary considerably.

The process of learning the technical aspects of flash photography and, for that matter, photography in general, is facilitated by an understanding and appreciation of the concept of trade-offs...everything is connected to everything else...nothing is free. It is reasonable to assume that there is some trade-off for every "benefit" in photography. In many ways this helps us understand photography. This concept first became clear to me when it was explained that the combination of f-stop and shutter speed in **Chart II-A** would be **identical**. The selection of one f-stop shutter speed combination over another only impacts the effect of depth of field **(Etc. # 12)** and camera/subject movement **(Etc. # 13)** and...**not exposure**.

This "reciprocity" is important to remember, as it is at the core of photography.

As you can see in **Chart II-A**, if you want a high shutter speed to "stop" a fast moving subject, it will generally require a wider aperture (low number) to provide correct exposure resulting in less depth of field. If you want a small aperture (high number) to increase depth of field, it will require a slower shutter speed to provide correct exposure. Not surprisingly, there is yet another trade-off to be considered if you want **both** fast shutter speed **and** greater depth of field. You could select a faster film or higher sensitivity. But, the trade-off is that faster films are generally lower in resolution and have a more course grain structure and high sensitivity settings in digital cameras generally generate more noise.

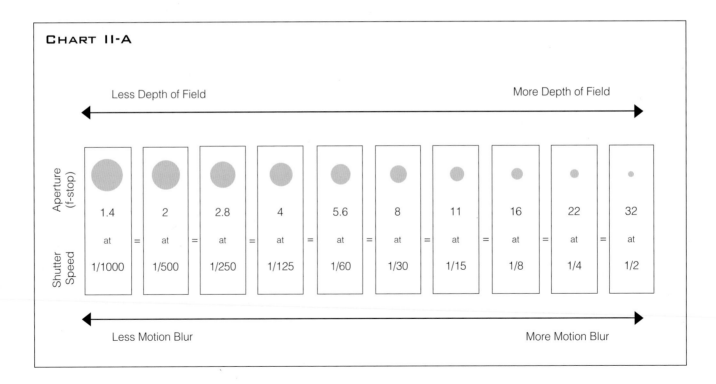

Here are a few of the trade-offs you will be working with in flash photography:

Desired Feature/Characteristic		Likely Trade-off
Wide Angle of Light Coverage	-	Reduced Maximum Distance
Softer Shadows	-	Reduction in Intensity
Increased Sophistication	-	Increased Cost
Extensive Options	-	Increased Size/Weight
High Sensitivity	-	More Noise
High Film Speed	-	Reduced Resolution
High Number of Images Per Disk	-	Reduced Resolution
High Shutter Speed	-	Reduced Depth of Field

… and the list goes on and on. Everything on your "wish list" comes at a price.

The importance of understanding trade-offs cannot be overstated. With each situation you must evaluate the trade-offs and how they relate to your objectives. **The key is to know what you are giving up to gain what you want and to understand and manage these trade-offs.**

TRADE-OFFS ON LOCATION

Let's say you are shooting party photos. Your priorities would probably be ease and speed of movement, dependability, catching the action.

You are probably not particularly concerned about light quality, shadows or a "natural" look. You might select on-camera direct flash, TTL (Through The Lens) center weighted metering. This combination will be the easiest, most foolproof way to accomplish your objectives. Of course, there are substantial trade-offs. Your subject will be unmistakably illuminated by a photographic flash coming from an unnatural direction (the camera), casting rather harsh shadows.

Each step you take to offset these negatives involves compromising or reconsidering your original priorities. You must determine the degree to which you are willing to modify your original priorities to improve the quality of light. For instance, you can employ bounce and/or diffusion techniques/accessories… but they reduce mobility and increase recycle time **(Etc. # 2 and Etc. # 3)**. You might use slow shutter speeds to record some ambient light, but that could result in some image blur and probably require rear curtain sync, which effects timing since the flash fires at the end of the exposure **(Etc. # 17)**. Again, it is up to you to determine what trade-offs are acceptable to achieve the desired results.

Say you are photographing a mother and child under low light conditions. Of course, you could simply set the camera at flash sync like the party photos and have your on-camera flash the sole source of light for the scene and ignore available light **(Photograph 2-A)**.

Or…after reading this book, your thought process might go something like this…

Let's see. To photograph this mother and child I believe I would like some soft, warm, moody, relaxing lighting. I'll have the light come from the side as if it were coming from a window so I'll take the flash off the camera and bounce it off that wall, or maybe use a gold reflector to warm the light to give the illusion of late afternoon **(Etc. # 14)**. Now, I need a little fill on the other side so I can see detail in the shadow areas. Maybe another reflector or a slave **(Etc. # 15)** with a gold bounce surface…set about 1 to 1 1/2 stops under the primary light exposure. Now I want the surrounding area, foreground and background to be just visible… maybe a stop below the primary lights. So I'll use a slow enough shutter speed to expose available light in this the area that is 1 1/2 stops under the flash exposure. Hmmm (after metering)… that is only a 15th of a second so I'll have to tripod the camera and keep the subject still **(Etc. # 16)**. Or, I could have them move during the exposure…the soft blur might be nice. I've got to be sure to use rear curtain sync **(Etc. # 17)** so that the blur will be behind the sharp image. Of course, I would have to be careful with my timing because now the flash will go off at the end of the exposure rather than the instant I depress the shutter **(Photograph 2-B)**.

This might not make complete sense to you right now, but it will when you finish this book. You will be amazed how quickly you will be processing that information and making the decisions necessary to create the image you want.

Everything you will learn from this book is designed to enable you to have this dialogue with yourself, like a football quarterback in the middle of a play...automatically.

Photograph 2-A: On Camera Direct Flash

Photograph 2-B: "In the Mood"

Flash...The MOST available light

CHAPTER III: THE BASIC RELATIONSHIP BETWEEN THE CAMERA, THE FLASH, AND THE SUBJECT

It is likely that you are using a flash that is considerably more sophisticated than the simple manual units we will begin our discussions with. However, understanding some basic technical information will help take the mystery out of what is happening when you are using your flash.

Let's look at the basic operation of a flash and how the camera and flash "talk" to one another. When the flash is turned on, internal capacitors are charged with energy drawn from the batteries. These capacitors instantaneously discharge this energy in the form of light as the flash is fired. When connected to a camera, the flash fires at the same time that the expose button is depressed and the shutter opens to expose the chip (film). Each camera has a shutter speed that is recommended for flash photography, generally ranging from 1/60th to 1/500th of a second. This speed is referred to as flash sync **(Etc. # 10)** and assures that the shutter in the camera will be open and the chip (film) will be exposed at the same time the

flash is fired. You may use a slower than recommended shutter speed but a faster than recommended speed could result in a portion of the frame being unexposed or underexposed.

The flash and camera are connected electronically in one of two ways: either via the "hot shoe," if the flash is physically mounted on the camera or via the remote cord, if the camera and flash are not physically connected **(Etc. # 16)**. **Photographs 3, 4 and 5** illustrate several types of connectors. Attaching the flash to the camera is more convenient, but obviously, the remote cord offers more flexibility with regard to flash location.

Now that we have the camera and flash in sync with each other, we must make adjustments to assure proper exposure. The built-in available light meter in your camera will not help because the duration of the flash is too short to obtain an accurate reading. The shutter speed is set at flash sync. Therefore, in a flash with only one power setting, the only remaining variable to

Photograph 3: Most cameras are equipped with "hot shoes" which allow for simultaneous mechanical and electrical connection.

Photograph 5: Some sync cords allow for full operation of all dedicated flash features.

Photograph 4: The flash can also be connected with a PC cord to the X-sync outlet of the camera. PC extensions are available.

control flash exposure is your aperture. Unfortunately, light falls off as the distance between the flash and subject increases. As a result, when using a manual flash, the aperture will need to be adjusted as this distance varies. **Photograph 6** is a typical scale that provides aperture settings at various distances. You locate the speed (ISO) of the film you are using or the digital sensitivity, the distance between your flash and subject, and set your aperture at the setting indicated.

Photograph 6: Typical Scale Indicating Aperture Settings At Various Distances With A Manual Flash

While this is fairly simple, it is also time consuming and cumbersome. Fortunately, automatic flashes eliminate the need for these constant recalculations **(Etc. # 8)**. With the flash and camera correctly set in an automatic mode, an average subject will be correctly exposed as long as you remain within the automatic operating range of your flash unit **(Etc. # 18)**. The operating range is essentially the area that is close enough so that the flash has enough power to illuminate the subject but not so close as to illuminate the subject too quickly for the flash to accurately process exposure information. Automatic operation is generally controlled by an electronic sensor on the flash that reads the light level reflecting back from the subject. This sensor controls the amount of light emitting from the flash and prevents the flash from illuminating the subject more than required for a correct exposure. In the automatic mode, the flash emits the correct amount of light to properly expose the subject at a given f-stop regardless of distance as long as you remain within the automatic operating range. Sometimes that will require all or virtually all the power that the flash has stored in its capacitors and other times it will only require a small percentage of the power available. Keep in mind that the exposure automation system of your flash evaluates exposure information in largely the same way as does your in-camera meter, only faster. It calculates the amount of light necessary to expose the scene at a reflectance level of 18%. If your scene should be brighter or darker than an average (18%) reflectance, then the automation system will strive to make it average. The automation system will strive to make both a snow scene and a black bear 18% gray. To accommodate these extreme subject circumstances, you will have to tell your automation system or trick it into overexposing the snow (which it is trying to make 18% gray) so that it reproduces as white and underexposing the bear (which it is trying to make 18% gray) so that it reproduces as black. Depending on your flash, you might make that adjustment with the aperture setting, sensitivity setting or, the easiest, if your flash is so equipped, with the +/- adjustment.

Chapter IV: Flash Unit Features to Consider

Manufacturers have developed numerous variations, embellishments and improvements on the automatic flash; but, the basic concept remains as described in the preceding chapter. These more sophisticated characteristics are designed (or should be designed) to enable the photographer to obtain desired results easier, faster and with greater predictability. Not all features will be necessary to meet your objectives. Each of us must select a flash that represents an appropriate balance between sophistication, simplicity and cost **(Etc. # 8)**.

Let's take a look at flash features. The list is general and in descending order of importance for the typical photographer (if there is such a thing). Also, we will not address cost considerations, as this factor is variable and subjective.

Power

Your flash should have enough power, calculated in guide numbers **(Etc. # 18)**, to use the digital or film sensitivity you have selected, at the distance you will be shooting, and at the aperture you want to use. If you have any doubt whether the unit can accomplish this, simply enter the data into the calculator on the flash. For instance, in **Photograph 7**, a flash with a guide number of 120 is set at ISO 100. If, for example, you were planning on shooting at f/8 at 18 feet, then this flash is not powerful enough for your purposes. Whereas in **Photograph 8**, a flash with a guide number of 160 with ISO set at 100 is powerful enough to shoot f/8 at 18 feet. In addition, virtually everything you do to improve the quality of the light: relocating, bouncing, diffusing, etc., will result in some light loss. Do not mislead yourself into thinking that a flash will become more powerful when you get it home; buy one that has the power you need or you will never obtain satisfactory results.

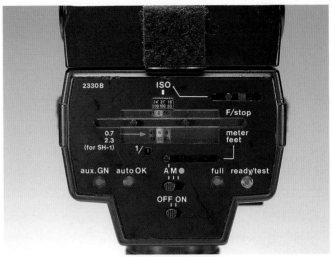

Photograph 7: Flash Unit With Insufficient Power
With the calculator dial set at ISO 100, this flash with a guide number of 120 will only enable you to shoot at a distance of 15 feet at f/8. Since you are planning on shooting at 18 feet, it is not powerful enough to meet your objectives. You must either modify your objectives or use a more powerful flash.

Photograph 8: Flash Unit With Sufficient Power
With the calculator dial set at ISO 100, this flash with a guide number of 160 will enable you to shoot at a distance of 20 feet at f/8. Therefore, it is powerful enough to meet your objectives.

AUTOMATIC OPERATION

Virtually all flashes have some degree of automatic operation and for most photographers it would not be advisable to consider a unit that did not. The simplest of these will provide you with the correct amount of light at a single preset aperture (f-stop) within a certain operating range. **Photograph 9** is such a unit; with the ISO set at 100, it provides you with automatic operation at f/4.

A variation on this unit is one in which there are multiple power settings that enable you to select one of several f-stop settings and the aperture on your lens to the f-stop that corresponds to the power setting on the flash. The unit will then provide consistent exposures over the entire automatic distance range. Essentially you are telling the flash to provide the correct amount of light needed to properly expose your subject at a selected f-stop. **Chart IV-A** indicates the

Photograph 9: Simple Automatic Flash With One Aperture Setting: This illustrates a simple automatic flash with one aperture setting. The combination of the ISO of the film or digital sensitivity selected and the power of the flash determines what the automatic f-stop will be. In this case it is f/4 and the automatic operating range will be from 3 to 15 feet.

CHART IV-A

Automatic operation at f/2.8

- Improved operating distance
- Shorter recycle time
- Limited depth of field

Automatic Operation at f/8

- Reduced operating distance
- Longer recycle time
- Improved depth of field

Primary Trade-Offs Resulting From Changing Power And Aperture Settings

relationships and trade-offs experienced as a result of changing power and aperture settings.

THROUGH THE LENS (TTL) METERING AUTOMATIC FLASHES

Most sophisticated cameras offer TTL flash metering which allows for the measurement of light to take place at the chip (film) plane. This feature can result in more consistent exposure for two reasons. First, the farther a flash is removed from a camera, the more discrepancy there might be between a light reading taken at the location of the flash and the location of the camera. Second, f-stop calibrations on a lens are the result of mathematical calculations and may not accurately reflect the exact actual light transmission characteristics of the lens. In other words, f/5.6 on one lens may not transmit **exactly** the same amount of light as f/5.6 on another lens. This could result in slight exposure variation when the light is not metered at the chip (film) plane. In addition, TTL metering compensates for filters, tele-converters, extension tubes and bellows. For those of you without TTL systems, this feature represents an increasingly popular refinement, not an absolute necessity.

Photographs 10 and 11 represent popular TTL flash/camera systems.

DEDICATED FLASH SYSTEMS

The development of the dedicated flash has resulted in sophisticated communication and cooperation between the flash and the camera. Many time-consuming calculations that were formerly done by the photographer can now be done automatically. This enhanced communication is made possible by the microprocessors and multi-pin connection between the foot of the flash and the hot shoe on the camera. The list of resultant features varies considerably from system to system, and is constantly expanding.

Photograph 10: Nikon D2H with a SB 800 Flash

Photograph 11: Canon EOS1N with a 540 EZ Flash

Here's an important note on all this automation. It is very easy to get bogged down in all the terminology such as Matrix TTL Balanced Fill Flash or some such thing. The engineers who, I suppose, write the instruction manuals seem to do a better job of describing what is happening than when or why we would want to use a feature and what will be accomplished by using that feature **(Etc. # 8)**.

As you review various features and modes, you really need only ask yourself a few questions to determine what the applications might be and if they are useful to you.

- Where is exposure control (metering) taking place...at the chip (film) plane (TTL) or on the flash itself?
- What is the pattern of the metering (spot, center weighted, matrix, etc.)?
- How is it controlling the relative intensity and balance of flash exposure and available light?

If you answer these questions about each "mode" that you are learning about, considering, or contemplating using, you can greatly simplify the process and take the mystery out of flash instruction books.

Hey, this is not rocket science...it just seems that manuals were written by rocket scientists! Listed below are some of the most popular automatic features:

- Viewfinder exposure signals (correct, under and overexposure information)

- Flash range preview (indication of the automatic operating range of the flash)

- Automatic fill flash (automatically balances the ratio between ambient light and fill flash)

- Coupled lens and flash head zoom (automatically adjusts the coverage angle of the flash to correspond to the focal length of the zoom lens)

- Automatic turn-off (automatically turns flash off after a certain period of inactivity)

- Metering alternatives (matrix, center weighted, spot, etc.)

Consult your dealer to see which features are applicable to the type of photography you do. Remember that possessing a piece of equipment that has these automatic features does not replace an understanding of how they work and what they can do for your photography.

AUTOFOCUS ASSIST

With the popularity of autofocus cameras have become flash units that emit an infrared beam allowing the autofocus feature to operate in total darkness. The beam is emitted as the expose button is partially depressed. As the beam strikes the subject, the lens focuses and the shutter is tripped, exposing the properly exposed and focused photograph. This feature has obvious advantages and works well with other automatic features.

HEAD ANGLE

When shooting on flash automatic (not TTL), in order to obtain an accurate exposure reading from the subject, the electronic sensor must be directed at the subject. Remember, it is instantaneously calculating the volume of light illuminating the subject and controlling the light emitting from the flash accordingly. If it is not pointing at the subject, it cannot operate properly.

This can become a problem when you do not want the flash head pointing directly at the subject. To employ the techniques discussed in this book and improve the quality of light over direct flash, it is important that you select a unit that allows you to direct the flash head and the sensor in different directions. Of course, if you are using TTL (through the lens) metering modes, the scene is always being metered through the lens at the chip (film) plane. **Photographs 12-A, 12-B and 12-C** illustrate several flash head/sensor relationships.

Photograph 12-A: Flash head and sensors are permanently pointing in the same direction. Automatic bounce photography is not possible with this unit.

Photograph 12-B: A rotating head enables the photographer to point sensor and head in different directions. Automatic bounce photography is possible with this design.

Photograph 12-C: A rotating/swivel head offers even more options regarding sensor/head direction.

BATTERY ALTERNATIVES

Your batteries are the source of power that recharges the capacitors in your flash. The ideal battery would be light, powerful, rechargeable, and inexpensive. However, many of these characteristics are, to a degree, mutually exclusive (remember, no free lunch!). Again, selection is dependent on your needs.

Chart IV-B compares the alternatives to help you make a decision. You may select several alternatives for different circumstances. These evaluations are the result of my personal field experience with each alternative.

There is no real "right or wrong" selection; suitability is entirely dependent upon the application. For instance, alkaline batteries work well for a "just in case" situation, where long-term cost and recharge ability are not as important as convenience, size and weight. Radio Shack makes an inexpensive battery tester that takes the guesswork out of determining battery

CHART IV-B	Alkaline	Rechargable Nicads	Nickel Metal Hydride	Deep-Cycle Lead Cells
Initial Cost	4	3	2	2
Long Term Cost	1	2	4	4
Recycle Time	2	1	4	4
Weight	3	3	4	2
Size	4	4	4	3
Rechargability	n/a	2	4	4
Dependability	3	2	4	4
Maintenance	n/a	2	2	3

Battery Comparison Chart   **0 = None/Bad   4 = Excellent**

condition. Deep-cycle lead cells and nickel metal hydride (i.e., Quantum batteries) are initially more expensive and heavier. However, short recycle times **(Etc. # 19)**, capacity, recharge ability, and long term cost effectiveness make them the choice for many wedding, P.R. photographers, press and other demanding professionals.

OTHER FEATURES

In addition to the primary characteristics reviewed above, other less universally applicable features should be considered. These features might prove very useful for your particular needs, so take the time to review them with your dealer.

You now have the basic information necessary to select a flash unit intelligently. You have learned what features are important to you; and, to a large extent, you are free to mix and match brands and models. For instance, a Nikon camera works fine with a Sunpak flash and a Quantum battery pack. If there is any question about compatibility, ask your dealer. It is possible that some features that are important to you are best obtained when using certain flash/camera combinations. I would, however, caution you against "bargain" off-brand equipment. It can both fail at the most inopportune moment and possibly damage other pieces of equipment.

Flash...The MOST available light

CHAPTER V: PUTTING IT TO USE

The information in Chapter IV enabled you to make an informed purchase of a new flash so let's get it out of the box and into your camera bag. I suggest you use alkaline batteries until you determine that your applications warrant one of the more sophisticated options.

As far as other accessories to help you employ the concepts and techniques that we have been discussing, you have a number of choices. There are two broad categories of accessories…stuff you take with you and stuff that is already at the location. Obviously, stuff already at the location is the easiest to use but you will have had more experience with the stuff you take with you and you have a clear idea of what you have to work with. I use a combination of the two.

One of the most useful techniques is to reflect or bounce the light off some nearby surface… usually a ceiling **(Etc. # 2)**. This is generally a huge improvement over direct flash because it creates a light source that is both larger and coming from a more natural direction **(Etc. # 5)**. Diffusing the light is effective too, but the chance of finding a piece of diffusion material on location is much more remote than finding a bounce surface **(Etc. # 3)**.

Of course, sometimes neither one is available and that is when you will be glad that you took some accessories with you. We designed the **LumiQuest**® line of flash accessories for this situation **(Etc. # 7)**. We made every effort to develop accessories that were effective, compact and cost effective.

There is nothing magical about these accessories; they employ the very principals that we have been discussing and elaborated on in **Etc. #'s 2, 3, 4, 5,** and **7**. You may prefer products offered by other manufacturers…and…if these are roughly the same size, they will produce similar results. Selection will depend largely on portability, method of attachment and personal preference.

All of these accessories are more portable and yes, because they are smaller, are less effective than larger studio softboxes and umbrellas. To think that a **LumiQuest® Big Bounce** or a Shell can yield the same results as a 4' Westcott softbox would be ridiculous. However, when these and other portable accessories are used correctly, they can represent a dramatic improvement over direct flash.

Because of our preferences and extensive experience with the **LumiQuest®** line, we will use these accessories exclusively in our examples. Keep in mind that it would be entirely reasonable to substitute the Westcott Micro Apollo for the **LumiQuest® SoftBox**, the Stofen Omnibounce for the **LumiQuest® UltraBounce** or even the Shell for the **LumiQuest® Big Bounce**.

So now, armed with an understanding of what makes flash so unnatural and unflattering and knowing what to do about it, you are ready to put it to good use. Based on what you intend to photograph, you should select a flash and appropriate accessories to go on location.

Of course, you can always slip that flash on the hot shoe, select an automatic mode and fire away…**but** that is not why you are reading this book.

PHOTO GALLERY*

Big Bounce Slightly off Camera

SoftBox on Camera

Pocket Bouncer with Gold Insert off camera.

Big Bounce behind subject directed at ceiling and serving as both background and backlighting.

Photo by Raymond Muzika

SoftBox on camera

Snoot off camera

SoftBox II on camera

Pocket Bouncer off camera

Ultrasoft on camera

* All of the images in the Photo Gallery were photographed with flash, using various **LumiQuest**® bounce and diffusion products as indicated under each image.

Misconceptions and Frequently Asked Questions

There are a number of common misconceptions which surface regularly in conversations with photographers. Here are a few of the most common:

I want to eliminate shadows.

Actually, eliminating shadows would generally produce a pretty boring scene. Shadows add depth, texture, and therefore, three dimensionality to a photograph. The key is to learn to manipulate and control shadows to accomplish the "look" you want.

A diffuser over the flash head will soften the shadows.

Yes, but only if the light is allowed to refract through the diffuser, creating a larger light source.

I don't need another flash; one is built into my camera.

Built-in flashes can be effective subtle fill to provide a catch light or fill harsh shadows. However, a built in flash embodies every unpleasant, unnatural characteristic generally associated with flash…small, harsh, unnatural direction and are prone to producing red-eye.

I can get the same results with a 1 ft. wide softbox as the larger 4 ft. studio models.

Unfortunately, this is not the case. While a 1 ft. wide softbox is many times the size of your flash head, your studio softbox is considerably larger…and the larger the light source, the softer the shadows.

Bare bulb (or the LumiQuest® UltraBounce or the Stofen Omnibounce) produces much softer shadows...I see the pros use them all the time.

These devices are light distribution devices and require surfaces such as walls and ceilings to bounce light back into the scene. Since they are not materially larger than the flash, they have very little impact on light quality in the absence of bounce surfaces. Yes, you often see photographers using these devices outdoors or in large rooms but it should be pretty obvious that illuminating your shoes or the photojournalist standing next to you will have little effect on the scene you are photographing **(Etc. # 24)**.

Why should I worry about lighting when shooting with digital, I can fix it in Photoshop®?

There is no question regarding the image enhancement and "fixes" possible using Photoshop®. However, Photoshop® is no replacement for getting it right in the first place. The closer the original image is to aesthetic and technical perfection, the easier your life will be. Not only will you save many hours of Photoshop® work, the less "manipulated" image will generally be preferable.

ETC. #1: FLASH AND DIGITAL IMAGING

As the world transitions to digital imaging, a lot of questions are raised regarding what impact this transition has on traditional imaging issues. Flash photography and lighting in general are no exception.

For the most part, light is light and shadows are shadows regardless of which media they are recorded on. Photoshop® and other image manipulation tools can definitely improve an image but nothing beats getting it right in the first place!

Many newcomers to digital imaging will notice its narrower latitude relative to negative film, more closely approximating color slide film. So, if anything, this requires that a bit more attention be paid to even light distribution.

The digital photographer has the considerable advantage of being able to view images immediately and make corrections and adjustments. However, this does not replace invaluable photographic skills such as composition, timing, framing, direction, use of color and of course, the impact of light and its many characteristics. In fact, the immediate feedback offered by digital imaging enables the photographer a greater opportunity to experiment with and fine tune lighting subtleties.

There is a law of physics that states, "the angle of incidence equals the angle of reflection." The effect of this law is that beams of light striking a reflective surface at a given angle will be reflected off that surface at an equal and opposite angle **(Illustrations A-1 and A-2).**

In photography this is important for two primary reasons. An understanding of the law helps you prevent unwanted reflections including "red-eye" **(Etc. # 22)**. Secondly, understanding this law enables you to direct light accurately for "bounce light" photography.

The composition of an object determines its reflective characteristics. This in turn affects, among other things, its color and tendency to absorb light energy in the form of heat or reflect that energy in the form of light. Dark objects tend to convert more light energy into heat and

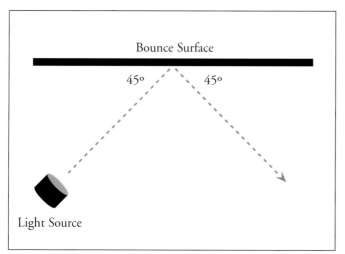

Illustration A-1

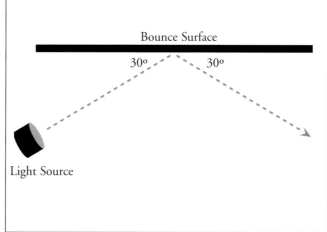

Illustration A-2

reflect less; conversely, light objects tend to convert less light energy to heat and reflect more energy in the form of light.

Using the Incidence/Reflection Law, you can direct the "bounced" light to illuminate the scene by adjusting the lighting instrument, the bounce surface, the subject or some combination of the three **(Illustrations B-1, B-2, B-3 and B-4)**.

There are several benefits of illumination with bounce flash. First, the bounce surface becomes the new and larger source of light for the scene. This larger light source provides more even illumination and softer shadows **(Etc. # 4)**. In addition, the bounce surface almost certainly represents a light source from a more natural direction than on-camera flash. Due to the greater distance that this light must travel and that some light is converted to heat in the bouncing process, a certain amount of light is lost **(Etc. # 18)**. As a result of this light loss, maximum operating distance of the flash will be reduced and, when shooting on manual, compensation must be made to assure correct exposure. When using flash automatic or TTL exposure, compensation is accomplished automatically; however, and again, maximum-operating distances will be reduced.

As mentioned earlier, the composition of a surface determines the wavelengths of light which are absorbed in the form of heat and those which are reflected in the form of light. It is the wavelength of those that are reflected that gives the object its color. As a result of this, any light reflecting from that object will be of that wavelength and therefore the color of the object itself. Simply put, if you reflect light off a colored surface, it will reflect light of that color. This is not necessarily a good thing or a bad thing but it is a fact that must be understood and dealt with accordingly.

To maintain normal color balance, care must be taken to assure neutral colored bounce surfaces, as the reflected light will be the color of the bounce surface **(Photographs 13-A, 13-B, 13-C and 13-D)**.

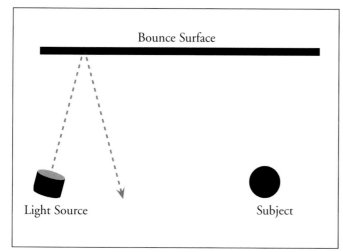

Illustration B-1: Bounce light misses subject

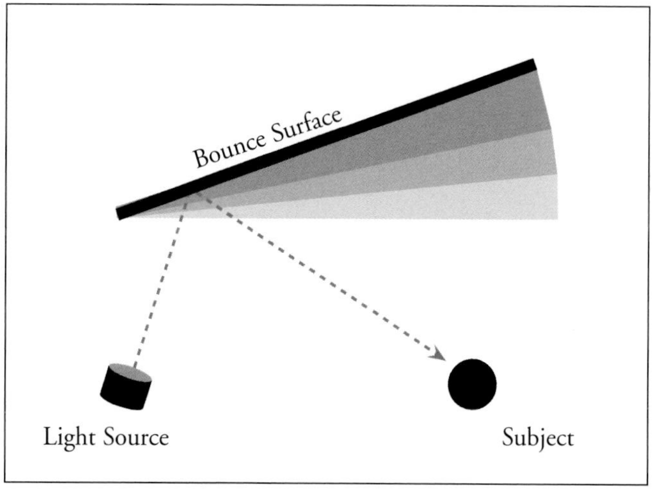

Illustration B-3: Move bounce surface

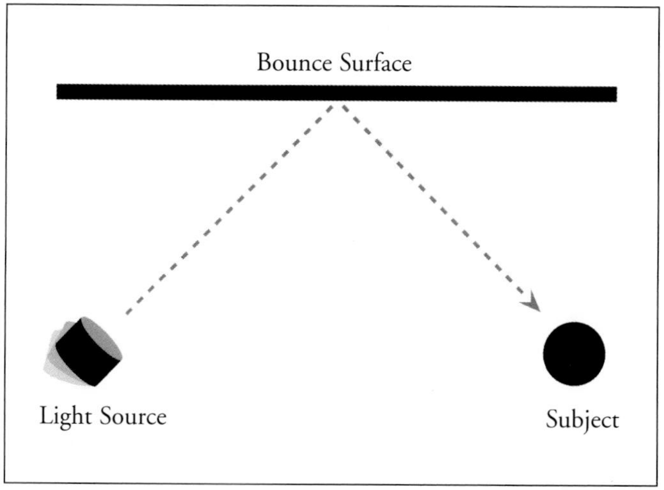

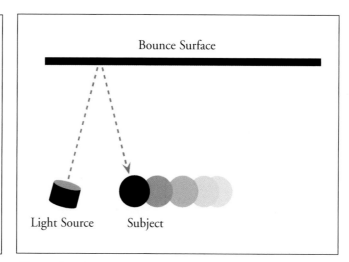

Illustration B-2: Move or redirect lighting instrument

Illustration B-4: Move subject

Photograph 13A: Neutral Surface

Photograph 13C: Red Surface

Photograph 13B: Green Surface

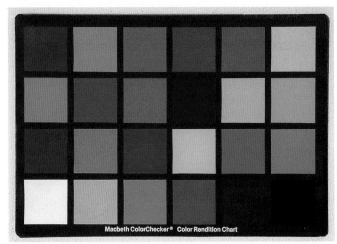

Photograph 13D: Blue Surface

The same principals apply when you want to avoid unwanted reflections. You must first identify reflective surfaces within the scene. These might be eyeglasses, highly polished items, windows and any number of other objects. Keeping in mind "the angle of incidence equals the angle of reflection", determine if the camera will "see" the light reflecting off a surface. If you determine that it will, you can either remove the reflective object from the scene completely, move the camera, move the light source or make some adjustment to the reflective object itself **(Illustrations C-1, C-2, C-3 and C-4)**.

There are also "dulling" sprays available; but generally, the most practical solution is an adjustment to assure that the camera lens cannot "see" the reflection.

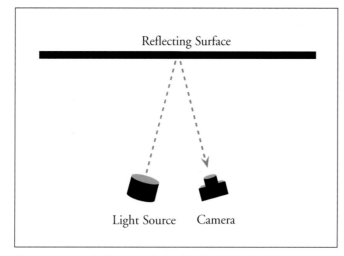

Illustration C-1: Camera "sees" reflection

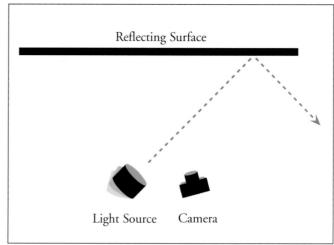

Illustration C-3: Move light source

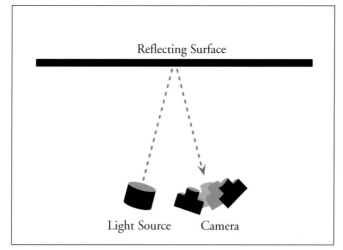

Illustration C-2: Move camera

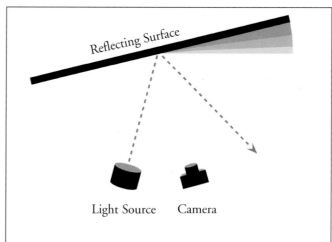

Illustration C-4: Move reflecting object

Etc. #3: Diffusion

Another effective technique to enlarge a light source is diffusion. As the light strikes a translucent material, it refracts through the material and that translucent surface becomes the new larger light source. Generally, and up to a point, the more diffuse the material is, the more the light will refract through the material creating a more even and larger light source. The trade-off for this is light loss in the form of heat. Various types of "softboxes" are commonly used and have the advantage of having bounce surfaces inside to redirect the light back into the translucent surface. The result is a brighter translucent surface than would result from the translucent material alone.

Just as a bounce surface absorbs some wave-lengths of light and reflects others, so does diffusion material. If you refract light through colored diffusion material, it will result in a significant color shift in the direction of the color of the diffusion material. Both bounce surfaces and diffusion material must remain neutral to avoid unwanted color shifts.

An important point needs to be made here… diffusing the light alone has negligible impact on shadow softness **unless** you allow the light to refract through the diffusion material to create that **larger** source of light. In other words, a piece of diffusion material roughly the same size as your flash head, placed over that flash head, would have virtually no impact on shadow softness. It would only reduce intensity of your flash by converting some of the light energy to heat **(Etc. #'s 4 and 24)**.

Flash...The MOST available light

Etc. #4: Light Source Size

Shadow softness is dictated almost exclusively by light source size. Given the same lighting instrument to subject distance, a larger light source will always produce softer shadows. If this were not the case, photographic studios the world over would not be equipped with large umbrellas and softboxes. This fact is indisputable and there are many ways we can use it to our advantage.

A shadow is the result of an object blocking the light from reaching the surface(s) behind it. If it completely blocks the light from reaching an area, then that area will be in deep shadow. If it doesn't block any of the light from reaching the surface, then that area will be fully illuminated. The area between the fully illuminated area and the completely blocked off area is what we are concerned with when we make efforts to "soften the shadows." A gradual transition from the fully illuminated area to the deep shadow area is generally referred to as a "soft shadow." An abrupt transition from the fully illuminated area to the deep shadow area is generally referred to as a "hard shadow."

The quality of these shadows is significantly impacted by the interaction between light source to subject distance and light source size. If a light source is very small relative to the subject, then it will cast a very large, hard shadow as in **Illustration D-1**.

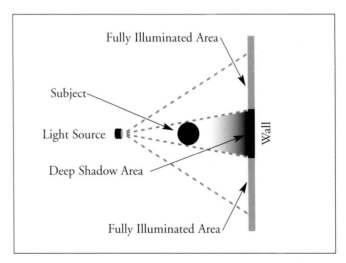

Illustration D-1: Small light source

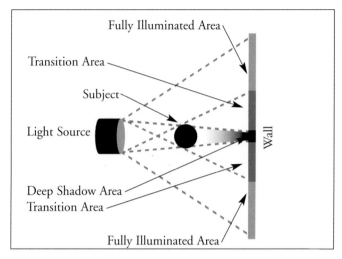

Illustration D-2: Medium light source

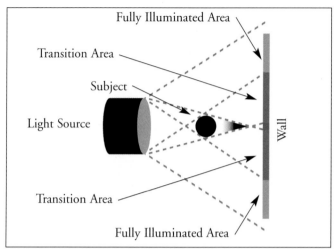

Illustration D-3: Large light source

If the light source is larger, then less area is in deep shadow and there is a larger area to provide a more gradual transition from deep shadow to full illumination as in **Illustration D-2**.

If the lighting source is even larger as in **Illustration D-3**, then all of the formerly deep shadow area is receiving significant illumination and the transition area becomes very gradual and very soft. Obviously, the size of the light source relative to the size of the subject casting the shadow impacts the ability of that subject to block the light, resulting in a shadow.

Light source to subject distance impacts shadow softness as well. In **Illustration D-4**, notice how increasing the distance reduces the transition area, which produces harsher shadows.

Essentially, the light is becoming a point source as it gets farther from the subject. To understand this concept consider the sun, a huge light source that is 864,000 miles wide, but it is a point source of light because it is 93,000,000 miles away from us, the subject.

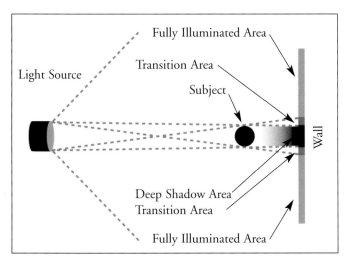

Fully Illuminated Area

Transition Area

Light Source

Subject

Wall

Deep Shadow Area
Transition Area

Fully Illuminated Area

Illustration D-4: Distant light source

These illustrations depict a very simplistic scene: a light source, a subject, and a wall. Understand that these principles apply to every element of the frame. That shirt collar, doorknob, sunglasses, hat brim, flower arrangement, or whatever, will be impacted. By softening the thousands of little shadows within the frame, you soften the entire look, not just the shadow on the wall behind the primary subject. Understanding the impact of these variables will help you make informed lighting decisions.

Flash...The MOST available light

Etc. #5: Direction

Generally speaking, if a subject is illuminated from a direction that could occur in nature, the observer accepts that source as believable and natural. Directionality is an issue in any lighting situation but it is particularly acute in flash photography because the starting location for the light source is "on-camera." Since rarely in nature is the observer the light source, relocating that light source is an important first step toward making it feel more natural. Directionality is one of several factors involved in creating the desired lighting mood **(Etc. # 11)**.

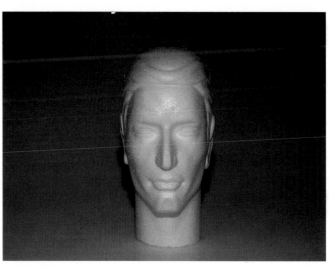

Photograph 14

Front Light

The light source is directly in front of the subject resulting in an even, yet flat, largely textureless look. Front lighting is safe for passport pictures but most would consider it lacking in interest and depth.

Photograph 15

SIDE LIGHT

Photograph 16

BACK LIGHT

The light source is on one side or the other of the subject. Long shadows emphasize the texture and three dimensionality of the subject at the risk of leaving some areas lost in deep shadow.

The light source is behind the subject, creating a bright rim of light around the subject. Back lighting can be dramatic when used skillfully under the right circumstances.

Photograph 17

TOP LIGHT

Photograph 18

BACKGROUND LIGHT

The light source is above the subject. Top lighting can be natural in that both the sun and indoor lighting usually comes from above the subject and it provides even illumination of the scene. However, some form of front or sidelight is usually needed to "fill" the shadows cast by the top light.

By illuminating the background, rather than the subject itself, a silhouette of the subject is created.

Flash...The MOST available light

Etc. #6: Uneven Illumination

One would conclude that the road to soft, even lighting would be to position a large light source as close to the subject as possible. This is true with regard to shadow softness. Both bouncing light and diffusing light generally result in more even left to right and top to bottom illumination… **but** only within the plane of correct exposure. Neither of these techniques has an impact on light fall off over distance. In other words, no matter how much larger and softer your light source becomes, the discrepancies between foreground and background exposure will be the same unless you intervene. There is an important law of physics that states "Light falls off at the inverse proportion of the square of the distance between the light source and the subject." As the light source to subject distance doubles or halves, light intensity on the subject increases or decreases by 2 stops. As a result, objects closer to the light source than the properly exposed subject (foreground) will be overexposed and objects farther from the subject (background) will be underexposed

(Illustration E-1). This is not as much of an issue for large, distant light sources, such as the sun, as it is when using a photographic flash. The reason for this is that the exposure difference in an object that is three feet from a flash and one that is eight feet from the flash is dramatic. Whereas the exposure difference between a subject 93,000,000 miles from the sun and 93,000,000 miles and five feet from the sun is obviously insignificant.

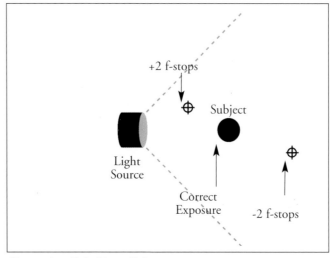

Illustration E-1: Close light source

As the lighting source to subject distance increases, the discrepancies between illumination levels for foreground and background objects are reduced **(Illustration E-2)** since the distance between these objects is a smaller percentage of the lighting source to subject distance.

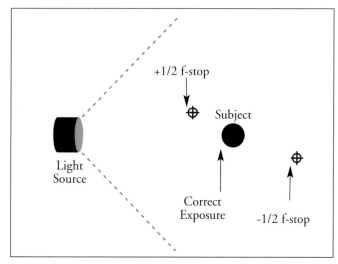

+1/2 f-stop

Subject

Light
Source

Correct
Exposure

-1/2 f-stop

Illustration E-2: Distant light source

There are several options to minimize the effect of light fall off. But, no surprise here, they **all** have trade-offs. In some cases, the trade-off is inconsequential. In other cases, it is completely unacceptable. This will, of course, depend on the situation and your objectives.

Here are the options for minimizing foreground/background exposure discrepancies:

• Rearrange the subjects to be more equidistant from the light source.
• Relocate your light source to be more equidistant from your subjects.
• Block off the light source selectively.
• Employ additional lighting instruments.

The potential compromises involved in these options should be pretty obvious and the only one that requires further explanation is employing additional lighting instruments **(Etc. # 15).**

Here are a few important trade-offs to be considered at this point:

• To enlarge the light source by bouncing and/or diffusing the light generally results in softer shadows but with a loss of intensity (power). To obtain the same level of illumination (exposure) requires more output from the flash.
• As a light source moves closer to the subject, the shadows soften; but there will be a greater discrepancy between the illumination levels of foreground and background objects.

• Conversely, as you move the light source farther from the subject, foreground and background objects will be more evenly illuminated; but shadows become increasingly harsher (remember the sun).

Obviously one of the most important lighting challenges facing the photographer is to select a light source of an appropriate size, placed at a distance from the subject that will produce both the desired shadow softness (transition area) and even illumination for all areas of the scene. This often means adjustments to the scene, the lighting instrument location, or both.

Over the last two decades, **LumiQuest**® has developed an effective, comprehensive line of photographic flash accessories. Our bounce and diffusion devices improve both digital and film flash photography for millions of professional and serious amateurs. The original **LumiQuest® Pocket Bouncer** remains the most popular bounce device in the world. Attached at a 45° angle to your flash head, the **Pocket Bouncer** enlarges and more evenly distributes the light while increasing the distance between the light source and the camera.

The **LumiQuest**® **80-20** is a variation of the **Pocket Bouncer** to be used when low, neutral ceilings are available. It allows 80% of the light to pass through and bounce off the ceiling while reflecting 20% forward to fill shadows cast by the ceiling bounce. The **80-20** is also a component of the **LumiQuest**® **ProMax System**, a six piece light modification kit. The system includes an **80-20** ceiling bounce device, white, gold and silver inserts as well as a removable frosted diffusion screen. **The ProMax System** enables the photographer to deal with a variety of different lighting situations on location, maximizing the potential of the shoe and handle mount flash unit.

The **LumiQuest**® **SoftBox** diffuses the light with the flash in the direct flash position. The light is softened and more evenly distributed as it passes through a center-weighted frosted diffuser. The unique design does not block exposure sensors or auto focus assist beams on most flashes.

The **LumiQuest**® **Mini SoftBox** is a compact version of the original **SoftBox**. While it is not quite as large (and therefore not as soft), its low profile is ideal for fast moving photographers such as photojournalists.

The full line of **LumiQuest**® flash accessories can be reviewed at **www.lumiquest.com**.

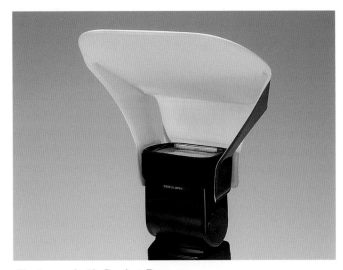

Photograph 19: Pocket Bouncer

Photograph 21: Mini SoftBox

Photograph 20: SoftBox

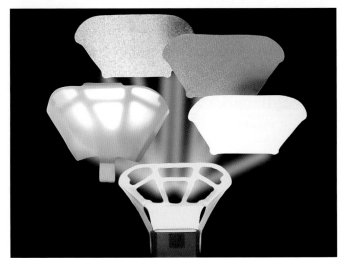

Photograph 22: ProMax System

Etc. #8: Camera/Flash Automation

Generally, the process of reviewing flash features in a manufacturers' instruction book consists of a list of terms, descriptions of what is basically happening technically, and then perhaps, a stab at an application for that feature. This probably makes more sense to the engineers who design the flash(es) than it does for the photographers who use them. We are going to review these features in reverse…actually in the way they were developed…in the way that the photographer actually used them.

Photographer **Problem/Objective/Activity**	**Engineer** **Automated Solution**
Constant recalculations were needed to compensate for changing flash to subject distances and therefore exposure differences.	**"Automatic exposure"** Flash automatically adjusts light output to correctly expose the subject at various distances.
Recalculations necessary to compensate for discrepancies between the light that is hitting the chip (film) and the metering that is taking place as some other location.	**"Through The Lens (TTL) Metering"** Exposure metering for both available light and flash takes place at the spot where the chip (film) is actually exposed, inside the camera at the chip (film) plane, after the light passes through the lens.

Photographer **Problem/Objective/Activity**	**Engineer** **Automated Solution**
Coordinating settings between camera and flash with regard to aperture, focal length, etc.	**"Dedicated Flashes"** Camera and flash actually communicate information to one another automatically.
Years of experience and many photographs enable a photographer to deal effectively with a variety of situations.	**"Matrix Metering" "Program Modes"** Various metering and program modes benefit from information stored in chips, simulating actual photographer experience.
Flashes are often used in low light conditions where manual focus is difficult and there is not enough available light for auto-focus.	**"Auto-Focus Assist"** Flash emits an infrared beam to enable low light focusing.

By understanding the problem being solved and therefore the application for an automatic feature, the photographer can more readily understand both the feature and if and when it should be used.

Reflective metering for both available light and flash exposure is accomplished by measuring the volume of light reflecting back from the subject.

AVAILABLE LIGHT exposure is controlled by a combination of how much time the chip (film) is exposed to light through what size opening (aperture). If a certain amount of light for a certain period of time results in correct exposure, then doubling one would require halving the other to obtain that same exposure **(Chart 9-A.)**

FLASH EXPOSURE is controlled by the intensity of the light in combination with what size opening (aperture). If a certain amount of light at a certain flash intensity results in correct exposure, then doubling one would require halving the other to obtain that same exposure. **(Chart 9-B).**

CHART 9-A

Time (shutter speed)		Volume (aperture)		Correct available light Exposure
1	x	X	=	X
1/2	x	2X	=	X
2	x	1/2X	=	X

Available Light Exposure

CHART 9-B

Power (setting on flash)		Volume (aperture)		Correct Flash Exposure
1	x	X	=	X
1/2	x	2X	=	X
2	x	1/2X	=	X

Flash Exposure

Therefore:
- Both available light AND flash exposure are effected by volume (aperture) adjustments.

Whereas:
- Adjusting shutter speed ONLY effects available light exposure
- Adjusting flash power ONLY effects flash exposure

Most dedicated flash/camera combinations have independent exposure (+/-) controls for available light and flash exposure control. These controls are a simple, fast way of varying the impact of available light and flash on the subject. At the (O) setting, both will be "balanced" at correct exposure. By reducing intensity some increment of (-), that light source will become increasingly secondary, reducing its impact on illuminating the subject, while the other light source correctly illuminates the subject at the (O) setting. A little experimenting with these (-) settings will enable you to select a balance that suits your objectives. I mentioned earlier that generally speaking I prefer fill flash 1-1 1/2 stops under available light. Generally, you will not use the (+) settings for average scenes since that would result in overexposure.

The (+) settings are useful when you are photographing very light scenes since the exposure automation is striving to render the scene 18% gray. By intentionally "overexposing" to some degree, the brides dress or snow scene will be rendered white rather than 18% gray.

9

Etc. #10: Sync Speed

Sync speed refers to the highest shutter speed possible when using a flash that still assures full exposure while the shutter is open. This generally varies from 1/60th to 1/500th of a second depending on the camera. If you exceed the sync speed, at least a portion of the image may not be fully illuminated by the flash. With most newer cameras this is not a problem since they will not allow you to take a flash photograph with a flash if the shutter speed is beyond sync speed. The primary advantage of a high sync speed capability is the option to use that higher shutter speed when combining your flash with high levels of available light such as fill flash in outdoor situations. If your sync speed is very slow, it will limit your options to very small apertures to expose available light properly, perhaps one that is beyond the capability of your flash.

You can however, select a shutter speed slower, even significantly slower than sync speed, and not effect the portions of the scene illuminated by the flash. When you select increasingly slower shutter speed, the portions of the scene illuminated by available light receive more exposure. In this manner, available light can approach and even exceed the level of illumination of the flash.

As shutter speeds lengthen, the possibility of subject or camera movement increases. This will result in a blur that may or may not be desirable. In addition, since the flash fires at the beginning of the slow exposure, the available light blur will occur after the sharp flash exposure. This will create an unusual blur in front of a moving subject which is generally considered unnatural and undesirable. Most sophisticated flash units have the capability to synchronize to the end of the exposure (rear curtain sync), which eliminates this problem **(Etc. # 17)**.

10

Flash...The MOST available light

Etc. #11 Lighting Moods

Being able to establish the desired mood with lighting is actually the objective of this entire book. Becoming technically competent with your flash is largely a means to this end. Essentially, creating the desired mood **IS** the point.

I suggest that you avoid "formula" lighting with pre-established ratios. Rather, learn to appreciate the effect of balancing available light and direction, fall off, light source, size, etc. I have developed an understanding of what various factors bring to a lighting scheme and simply use these components in different combinations to craft the "look" and "feel" that I want. Of course, there is a degree of repeatability and you develop strategies that work well for certain subjects. I also enjoy bringing something special to each scene where possible.

Here are the most important components involved in establishing the mood of your scene:

1. Lighting direction **(Etc. # 5)**.
2. Quality of the shadows (harsh or soft) **(Etc. # 4)**.
3. Contrast and evenness of illumination **(Etc. # 6)**.
4. Color balance **(Etc. # 14)**.

Your life as a photographer should involve an ongoing appreciation for the characteristics of different environments. By combining these observations with the information in this book, you can create the moods you desire at will… a "look" that is both appropriate and unique.

11

Etc. #12: Depth of Field/Perspective

Depth of field refers to the area in front of and behind the object focused on which is still in acceptable focus. Of the area in focus, approximately 1/3 will be in front of the point of critical focus, 2/3 will be behind it.

At a given subject to camera distance, lens focal length and plane of focus, **aperture** is the only adjustment that will impact depth of field.

- The lower the f-stop # (larger the opening), the shallower the depth of field. **(Photograph 23)**
- The higher the f-stop # (smaller the aperture), the greater the depth of field. **(Photograph 24)**

There are some common misconceptions regarding depth of field, lens focal length and perspective. For instance:

Photograph 23: f/4

Photograph 24: f/11

With a long lens at 7', depth-of-field can be rather shallow, with both foreground and background objects out of focus **(Photograph 25)**. It is generally accepted that a wide angle lens results in greater depth-of-field. This is true **(Photograph 26)** and is further evidenced by its enlargement **(Photograph 27)**. However, if you reduce the subject-to-camera distance so that the primary subject is roughly the same size with the wide angle as it was with the long lens, the depth-of-field remains largely the same **(Compare Photographs 25 and 28)**. Of course, perspective is dramatically different due to the reduced subject-to-camera distance.

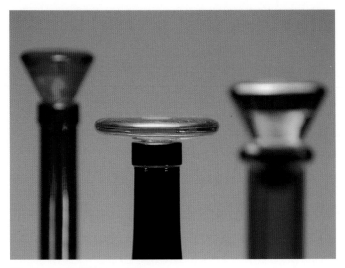

Photograph 25: Long lens

It is also generally accepted that a long lens "compresses" elements in a frame and that a wide angle lens "separates" or exaggerates the distance between foreground and background objects. Actually, that is not the case. It is the subject-to-camera distance, not focal length that effects perspective. Note that perspective is identical in images taken with wide angle and long lenses as long as the subject-to-camera distance remains constant **(Photographs 25 & 27)**.

I mention these misconceptions not because they are unique to flash photography, but because they are so common. It is obviously important to understand that the impact of changing focal length and/or subject-to-camera distance extends well beyond image size. Once again, managing and controlling trade-offs is necessary to create the images you want.

12

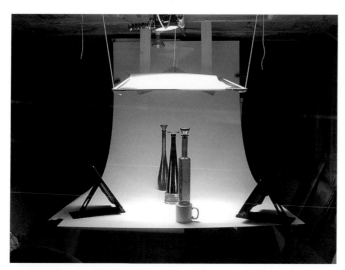

Photograph 26: Wide angle lens at 7'

Photograph 28: Wide angle lens at 18"

Photograph 27: Enlargement of wide angle lens Photograph 26. (Image degradation due to enlargement).

If a subject moves visibly during an exposure, it will be recorded as a blurred image. The "smearing" is from its position at the beginning of the exposure to its position at the end of the exposure.

For available light exposure, at a given shutter speed, if the camera or subject does not move perceptibly during the exposure, the motion is considered "stopped" and therefore "sharp." And conversely, the image is not considered sharp if it moves perceptibly during the exposure. This, of course, varies considerably from subject to subject. A speeding auto might be blurred at a 1/500th of a second whereas a relatively static person might be sharp at 1/30th of a second. Also, if a subject is moving left to right or right to left, it will move considerably farther (more blur) than if it were coming directly at or away from the camera. Here are some **VERY** rough guidelines for shutter speeds to stop moving subjects.

- $1/1000^{th}$ Auto Race
- $1/500^{th}$ Sports Event
- $1/125^{th}$ Human Conversation
- $1/60^{th}$ Wide Group Shot
- $1/30^{th}$ Camera Movement with standard lens

If the entire image is blurred consistently, it is generally due to camera movement. If the scene remains sharp, except for specific subjects, the blur is due to the movement of those subjects.

Depending on the output level of the flash, duration of the illumination can range from about $1/350^{th}$ of a second to $1/10,000^{th}$ of a second. As a result, the flash can be very effective at "stopping" most action. Essentially, the duration of the exposure is so brief as to not record visible movement of most subjects or the camera.

Generally, if slower shutter speeds (slower than $1/60^{th}$ to $1/30^{th}$ of a second) are used to allow for available light to impact exposures, it might be necessary to tripod the camera. This will only eliminate the effect of camera movement but will not effect blur as a result of subject movement during the exposure or flash exposure sharpness. Camera/subject movement during exposure combined with flash can produce some very interesting effects.

Here are a few interesting techniques you might want to consider:

• Use a very slow shutter speed to record the available light scene. Moving subjects will be either blurred, ghosts or possibly, even completely disappear while the flashed image will be correctly exposed and sharp. This is due to the fact that the moving subject never appears long enough at any point to receive enough exposure to record as a sharp image. The portion of the frame illuminated by the flash is both sharp and properly exposed **(Photograph 29).**

• Hand hold the camera and pan with the moving subject using rear curtain sync **(Etc. # 17)**. The available light exposed surroundings will be blurred horizontally while flashed subject will be sharp, properly exposed but with a "ghost" around it **(Photograph 30).**

Photograph 29

Photograph 30

13

Etc. #14: Color Temperature

In photography, the color differences in light are calculated in degrees Kelvin…generally referred to as "color temperature." The human eye (coupled with the brain) perceives substantial variations in color as normal and acceptable. Digital and film recording processes however, are much more sensitive to these variations. Color on the Kelvin scale range from the warmest (candlelight) at approximately 2000°K to the coolest (blue sky) at approximately 10,000°K An overcast sky and the electronic flash are both about 6000°K and that is approximately the color balance of daylight film.

Light sources that are warmer than daylight (late afternoon sun) will register approximately 3500°K and will be reddish gold. Shade under blue skies will be cooler than daylight and can be even bluer.

Flash is color balanced for daylight and its unaltered light will be acceptably color balanced when combined with daylight. However, as

Chart 14-A

Approximate Kelvin Temperature	Source
10,000	Blue Sky
5,500-6,000	Electronic Flash/ Average Daylight
3,400	Photo Floods
2,500	Household Tungsten
2,000	Candlelight

detailed in **Etc. # 2** and **Etc. # 3**, bounced or diffused light will "pick up" the color of the bounce surface or diffusion material. If you are to maintain color balance, these materials must be neutral in color.

Generally speaking, especially if you are photographing human skin tones, warmer light is preferable over cooler light. Most of us would prefer to look tanned rather than dead. In addition, any portion of the image that is illuminated by available light will be subject to the color shifts indicated in **Chart 14-A** when recorded on daylight film or a digital camera with white balance set on flash or daylight.

Here is how color balance can affect your flash photography in real life:

• You are shooting a casual portrait at sunset on a beach. The golden tones typical of that time of day make for a beautiful background but the subject is back lit and in deep shadow. Fill flash balances the subject with the sunset but loses the warmth of the scene. By bouncing the flash off a gold surface, the sunset mood of the scene is maintained **(Photographs 31 and 32).**

Interesting effects can be accomplished by using colored filters over either the camera lens, the flash, or both. If a color filter is used over the camera lens, it will impact the entire image. If a colored filter is used over the flash, it will impact only that portion of the image illuminated by that flash.

Photograph 31: Neutral colored bounce surface

Photograph 32: Gold colored bounce surface

• The scene is illuminated by fluorescent fixtures and without filtration it has a green cast **(Photograph 33)**. With white balance set to fluorescent or a 30 magenta filter (30M) on a film camera, the color balance improves but the subject's face is in shadows and lacks "snap" **(Photograph 34)**. By leaving white balance set to fluorescent or a 30 magenta filter AND using fill flash with a 30 green filter (30G) on the flash, the flash color balances with the fluorescent fixtures and both are filtered at the camera. The result is both more accurate color and improved lighting **(Photograph 34)**.

Photograph 34: Fluorescent light with a 30M filter-no flash

Photograph 33: Unfiltered fluorescent light

Photograph 35: Fluorescent light with a 30M lens filter and a 30G filtered fill flash

15

Many scenes can be illuminated more successfully with a multiple flash setup. Usually the role of the additional flash is to fill shadows and generally illuminate areas not reached by the primary flash. If you have a little more time and equipment, the results are well worth it (**Photograph 36**). Care must be taken not to create multiple shadows from different directions. These "cross-shadows" tend to be both unattractive and unnatural. Synchronizing two or more flash units is relatively simple, requiring the addition of what is called a "slave" unit. These devices come in a variety of sizes and shapes with connections for most flash units. **Photographs 37, 38 and 39** illustrate several popular models and configurations. In addition, some flash units have built-in "slave" compatibility to facilitate multiple flash photography.

Regardless of which unit you select, the basic purpose and operation are the same. The primary flash automatically tells the slave unit to fire the secondary flash(es). The actual slave receiving unit and its corresponding flash are collectively referred to as the "slave." The most popular and least expensive slaves operate with photocells that are activated by the white light from the primary flash. Since photocells operate by line-of-sight, it is important that they "see" the flash that is to activate them. Under these circumstances, quality photocell slaves work fine unless there are other photographers using flash in the area. In order not to have your slaves being activated by other photographers, you

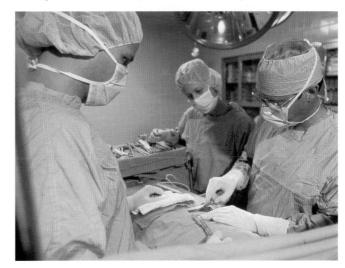

Photograph 36: Multiple Flash Setup

must use either hardwired slaves, which can be a significant inconvenience, or use either radio or infrared slaves. All radio and many infrared slaves operate on discreet channels, which leave them unaffected by any flash activity not operating on that channel. The radio slave is your best choice if your work might require setups that do not allow for line-of-sight between the transmitter and its receiver such as in multiple room situations. The infrared slave is your best choice in situations likely to have significant and nearby electronic or FM interference that could effect operation.

Photograph 38: Quantum Radio

Photograph 37: Wein Infrared

Photograph 39: Vivitar Photo Cell

Etc. #16: Camera/Flash Support

Removing a flash from the camera is an important step towards having the light that illuminates your image emanate from a more natural direction. If it is a manual or automatic flash, you can remove it physically from the hot shoe and leave it connected with a remote sync cord. By using a sync cord with your dedicated flash, you can remove it physically from the camera and still retain all dedicated capabilities.

Once you have removed the flash, you have several options for how to support it. The easiest is to simply handhold the flash while holding the camera with the other. The flexibility of this technique has the obvious limitation of running out of hands to operate controls on both the flash and the camera. Many professionals use a flash bracket to support their flash. This is a significant improvement over on camera flash especially when it comes to reducing red-eye **(Etc. # 22)**. But, the light is still basically from the direction of the camera, which tends to be less natural. The absolute best way relocate a flash off camera is to simply hand it to an assistant; but, obviously, there is not always one available.

Although it is a bit more cumbersome, I prefer a light stand or a tripod for relocating the flash or multiple flashes. If the sync cord is inconvenient, I use a slave unit **(Etc. # 15)** to activate the flash. That slave can be operated by the pop up or small flash at the camera, serving solely that purpose or also as subtle fill for the primary flash.

| FLASH...THE MOST AVAILABLE LIGHT

Etc. #17: Rear Curtain Sync

Rear curtain sync mode is one of those wonderful technical advances that make it absolutely simple to do something automatically that is very difficult to accomplish manually.

Under "normal" circumstances your flash is fired the moment you depress the shutter, regardless of the shutter speed. This works just fine at sync speed. The problem arises when you are using slower shutter speeds and there is subject and/or camera movement **after** the flash fires. The result is a "stopped" sharp image with a ghost image in **front** of the subject due to the movement that occurred after the flash was fired. This generally looks rather strange. It would be much more appealing to have the ghost image trailing the sharp image. To accomplish this, the flash needs to be delayed and made to fire just before the shutter closes and the exposure is over. Rear curtain sync accomplishes this automatically. You might wonder why you wouldn't use rear curtain sync all the time. Well, there is one drawback...the flash does not fire when you depress the shutter button; it fires just before the end of the exposure. This can result in significant timing problems **(Photographs 40 and 41).**

Photograph 40: Front Curtain Sync

Photograph 41: Rear Curtain Sync

Etc. #18: Operating Range/Light Loss/Exposure Metering

Operating Range

Generally the operating range of a flash is determined by its power. The guide number is the most widely accepted method of quantifying the power of "camera mount" or "hand held" photographic flash units. The guide number is determined by the following formula (most commonly calculated at ISO 100):

$$\frac{\text{Guide \#}}{\text{Distance}} = \text{f-stop}$$

The operating range can be significantly impacted by modifying the light (bouncing, diffusing, colored gels, etc.).

Light Loss

Essentially with every technique employed to manipulate and improve the quality of the light, there is some "light loss." This occurs primarily for one of two reasons. First, as light strikes a surface, some of its light energy is converted to heat, which is transferred to and dissipated by that surface. Second, if the light has to travel a greater distance to reach the subject, then it will lose its intensity at the inverse proportion of the square of the distance. If you are using a manual setting on your flash, you must compensate for that light loss either with your aperture setting or the output of your flash. In other words, if you know that the technique or device you are using results in a 2 stop "light loss," then you need to open up your aperture 2 stops to compensate and avoid underexposure. If you are using an automatic flash or exposure control, the flash will compensate for the light loss by outputting enough additional light to properly expose the subject. For instance, if a subject is 8' from the flash, and the light is being bounced off a 9' ceiling, the light will travel approximately 12' to reach the subject **(Illustration F)**. This additional distance must be considered the distance to the subject when shooting on manual. You should also open up approximately one additional stop to compensate for the light lost in the form of heat when the light strikes the bounce surface (the ceiling). The limitation would be if the flash did not have enough power to compensate for the light loss resulting from the technique or device. It is obviously more accurate to use a flash meter or a flash with automatic or TTL exposure capabilities. If you pay attention to the "Auto OK" features of your flash or flash/camera combination, they will indicate if your flash has reached a point at which it does not have enough power to properly expose the subject at the aperture that you have selected. At that point you must select a wider aperture, move closer to the subject, use a higher sensitivity setting, faster film or reconsider the use of the technique or device which is resulting in the light loss.

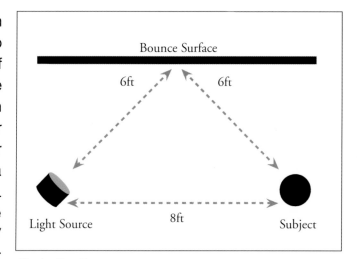

Illustration F

FLASH METERING

With the reliability and sophistication of most quality electronic flash units, consistent results can be obtained using the manual scales and automatic features to establish correct exposure. However, a flash meter offers an additional level of control and assurance. While they can be rather expensive, they can save time, film and reduce aggravation. A meter will tell you if proper levels of that "invisible" light is reaching all areas of the scene. It is particularly useful if control of the light is critical. In some cases, you might want to test your setup with a meter before shooting the assignment on automatic, just to make sure the automatic features are operating correctly. A variety of flash meters are available, depending on your needs.

Etc. #19: Flash Recycle Time

Each time you fire your flash, power stored in the capacitors is drained, providing that instantaneous burst of energy in the form of light. It takes some time for the capacitors to recharge with power drawn from the batteries. This process is referred to as recycling. Recycle time refers to how long it takes for the capacitors to be recharged so that the flash is ready to deliver a full power flash. Understanding the factors that effect recycle time can help you anticipate and deal with potential problems in advance.

Essentially three factors effect recycle time. First is the design of the flash itself. Check the specifications before you buy the flash to assure that recycle times are acceptable for your applications.

Second, the amount of "capacitor draw down" resulting from firing the flash. If you use only a portion of the power stored in the capacitors, they can recycle faster than if you drained them completely with a full power flash. Several factors impact the amount of power used and the resultant "capacitor draw down."

• Smaller apertures
• Greater flash subject distances
• Light modification (primarily bouncing and diffusing)

The third factor is battery selection and condition. Selection is covered in **Chart IV-B** (page 32). In addition, fresh disposable and fully charged rechargeable batteries will provide faster recycle times.

19

Flash...The MOST available light

Lighting a large space with small flash units can, at first, seem to be a daunting task. It is actually pretty simple. You should begin with metering available light and evaluating its color. Often available light sources are a combination of color (i.e. daylight, fluorescent, mercury vapor etc.). Since few facilities were designed to make life easier for photographers, the simplest approach is to meter available light and expose some amount (usually 1 stop) below your correctly exposed flashed subject. There is nothing magical about this 1 stop discrepancy. You might prefer 2 stops, 1/2 stop, or whatever. If adequate time is available, additional flashes (slaves) **(Etc. # 15)** can be used to highlight and emphasize other subjects within the frame. It is not unusual to have daylight, tungsten, mercury vapor and fluorescent in the same environment. While it may be out of the question to gel or overpower all of these light sources, properly color balanced primary subject(s) will go a long way towards being acceptable to the viewer. Indeed, color shifts throughout the frame can actually add depth and visual interest **(Photographs 42 and 43).**

Photograph 42: Large area/small flash(es)

Photograph 43: Large area/small flash(es)

Etc. #21: Exposure Compensation

The operating distance of your flash is reduced due to the power loss resultant from utilizing bounce and diffusion techniques. If you are shooting on manual, you must compensate for this loss by using the appropriate wider aperture. However, your **automatic exposure features remain entirely operational** because, if the electronic sensor on your flash has not been blocked (or you are using TTL), it reads the level of the light reflecting back from the subject **(Etc. # 9)**. The sensor does not know that you have modified the quality of the light; it only sees intensity. Therefore, it exposes the subject correctly as long as the sensor can still "see" the subject and you remain within the new, reduced maximum operating distance.

While I use a flash meter when time and circumstances allow, I often rely on the automatic features of my flash. Many of the examples in this book were photographed with the flash(es) in the automatic mode. Therefore, regardless of what you have done to modify the light, if you are shooting on automatic your AUTO OK LIGHT (or equivalent) must indicate correct exposure. If not, you must select a different automatic operating setting until it does. **Photographs 44 and 45** illustrate typical AUTO OK LIGHT examples. If your flash does not indicate correct exposure, you must use either a wider aperture, higher sensitivity setting (faster film), a more powerful flash, or change your setup, for you are attempting to operate beyond the automatic range of your equipment and the result will be underexposure.

Photograph 44: Metz

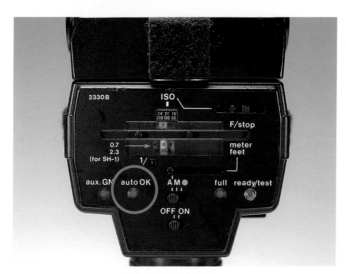

Photograph 45: Sunpak

ETC. #22: RED-EYE

Virtually every photographer has experienced the red pupils that can add a demonic look to even the most flattering portrait. This problem is the result of light reflecting off the concentration of blood vessels in the subject's retina. It is most noticeable with a concentrated light source such as an on camera photographic flash since the camera can "see" a significant portion of the light reflecting off the retina **(Illustration G-1).**

As the distance between the camera and the flash increases, red-eye becomes increasingly less noticeable since the camera cannot "see" the light reflecting off the retina **(Illustration G-2).**

However, even with this greater distance between the camera and the flash, red-eye becomes increasingly objectionable as subject-to-camera distance increases. Notice that as the angle of view converges, the camera can "see" an increasingly greater portion of the light reflecting off the retina **(Illustration G-3).**

Dilated pupils in low ambient light where flash is often used can aggravate the problem, as can larger pupils typical of children or pets.

Since it is impossible to change the subject's age and perhaps even the ambient light level, the most logical solution is usually to adjust the distance between the camera and the flash. This can be accomplished by either placing the flash off-camera on a tripod or, for more mobile situations, on a flash bracket such as a Stroboframe **(Photographs 46 and 47).**

Red-eye reduction modes emit a series of pre-flashes, causing the eyes to constrict, theoretically reducing red-eye. I am not a big fan of this option. It is not particularly effective, it is distracting, uses battery power, and effects timing.

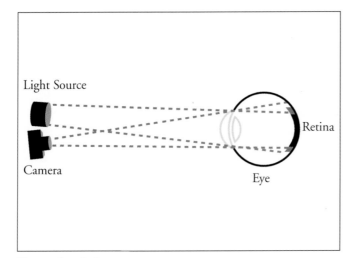

22

Illustration G-1

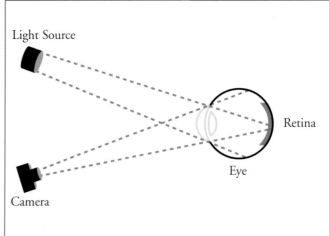

Illustration G-2

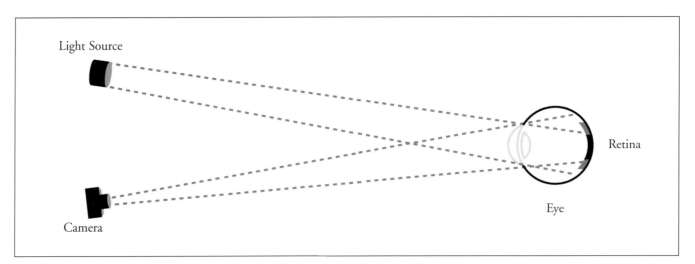

Illustration G-3

Photograph 46: On-camera flash

Photograph 47: Off-camera flash with SoftBox

Etc. #23: Digital Sensitivity/Film Selection

Sensitivity selection for your digital camera for the most part parallels film ISO selection. They both impact shutter speed and aperture settings with the same effect on subject/camera movement and depth of field. With film, a higher sensitivity results in increased grain and with digital, a higher sensitivity results in more noise.

Film selection has always been a matter of trade-offs, the most significant of which is film speed.

- Slower films - finer grain
- Faster films - courser grains

In addition, there are some personal preferences, usually in the areas of color saturation. I suggest that you find a few films which you like, get to know them well and stick with them.

Here are some guidelines:

- When shooting outdoors, you have to be cautious not to select a film that requires settings (both aperture and shutter) that make it difficult or impossible to use fill flash techniques. On a bright day, at sync speed, the aperture required for correct available light exposure may be so small as to require more light than your flash can deliver, even on full power.
- The opposite can be the case under low light conditions indoors. The film might not be fast enough to record available light images without unwanted ghosting blur due to subject movement resulting from very slow shutter speeds.

A good but very general rule of thumb would be as follows:

Outdoors   -   ISO 200 or less (slower)
Indoors   -   ISO 200 or more (faster)
Low Light -   ISO 400 or more (faster)

With regard to digital images, quality settings are not standardized and vary from one manufacturer to another. However, the following in a good rule of thumb for output applications.

CHART 23-A

Resolution			Megapixels	Print Size
640 x 480	(1,000,000)	=	0.3	3" x 4"
1280 x 960	(1,000,000)	=	1.2	6" x 8"
1600 x 1200	(1,000,000)	=	2.0	8" x 10"
2048 x 1536	(1,000,000)	=	3.2	10" x 13"
2272 x 1704	(1,000,000)	=	4.0	11" x 15"
3072 x 2048	(1,000,000)	=	6.3	13" x 20"

Chart courtesy of Paul Vaughn, www.graphicsguy.org

For e-mail applications, a resolution of up to 800 x 600 would be reasonable and manageable.

For years photographers have employed a technique referred to as "bare bulb" lighting. Essentially, it involves removing the directional reflector from the type of flash which uses a protruding bulb (Lumedyne, Norman, Sunpak 120J and Quantum Q flash are the most popular). By removing the directional reflector, the light is no longer directional and concentrated. Rather it is distributed over 180° or more. The **LumiQuest® UltraBounce** and StoFen Omnibounce are accessories which, when attached to the head of a conventional flash, accomplish similar objectives. The purpose is to bounce the light off nearby walls and ceilings producing soft, natural light. The technique is entirely dependent on the nearby walls and ceiling reflecting the light back into the scene. Since the walls and ceilings become the new and much larger light source(s) this technique can be very effective **(Illustration H-1).** However, without those surfaces to redirect the light, any light which is not pointed at the subject simply dissipates and has no impact on the photograph. While you may see photographers utilizing these devices and techniques in large rooms or even outdoors, it is a pointless waste of batteries and recycle time. Any illumination of areas outside the frame obviously has no impact on the scene unless that area bounces light back into the photographed area of the scene **(Illustration H-2).**

In addition, since the bare bulb represents a light source no larger than the original flash, shadows are not materially softened **(Etc. #4).**

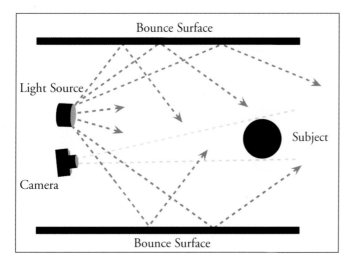

Illustration H-1: Subject illuminated by bounced light

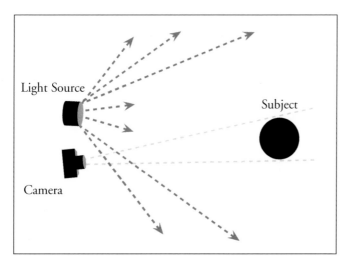

Illustration H-2: Light is not redirected to illuminate subject

Etc. #25: Other Flash Accessories (Portable Reflectors/Teleflash, Etc.)

Portable Reflectors

There are several portable, collapsible reflectors that are suited to fast moving flash work. These are available through a number of manufacturers. I use the compact model made by Westcott. It is 12" in diameter, folds to 4" and is available in silver, gold and white surfaces.

Teleflash

For telephoto flash work, there are several accessories that use a Fresnel lens to concentrate the beam of light from your flash and effectively extend its operating distance. These devices are most often used as fill for available light wildlife photography. George Lepp and Leonard Rue III make two of the most popular models. Due to the fact that the lens and the flash are so close together, care must be taken as red-eye is difficult to avoid with this set-up **(Etc. # 22).**

Flash...The MOST available light

GLOSSARY

APERTURE
The variable iris diaphragm in the lens which controls the light striking the film. The aperture is calibrated in f-stops, with a high number representing a small opening and a low number representing a large opening. For the purposes of photography, aperture and f-stop are used interchangeably.

CHIP
More accurately known as the CCD (Charge-Coupled Device), it is a grid of light sensitive sensors in your digital camera. The CCD essentially is the "digital film" that enables your digital camera to record an image.

BELLOWS
A mechanical interface between the camera body and the lens allowing for greater image control such as perspective adjustments and close-up focusing.

HOT SHOE
An electrical-mechanical connection between the camera and the flash which allows the camera to support the flash and communicate with it.

ISO
ISO is the International Standards Organization system of standardizing a film's speed or sensitivity to light. It expresses this sensitivity in terms of ASA and DIN. ASA is an abbreviation for the American Standards Association and is a system of standardizing a film's sensitivity to light. DIN is an abbreviation for Deutsch Industrial Norm, the European system for standardizing a film's sensitivity to light.

SYNC CORD
An electrical connection between the camera and the flash. Its functions may be as simple as firing the flash when the shutter is depressed or as complex as required to maintain full dedicated automation.

Flash...The MOST available light

PRODUCT INFORMATION

Products featured or mentioned in this book were provided to **LumiQuest**® by the following manufacturers and distributors:

Bogen Photo Corporation
www.bogenphoto.com
565 East Crescent Ave.
Ramsey, NJ 07446-0506
Tel: (201) 818-9500

Canon U.S.A.
www.usa.canon.com
One Canon Plaza
Lake Success, NY 11042-1113
Tel: (516) 328-5000

HP Marketing Corporation
www.hpmarketingcorp.com
16 Chapin Road
Pine Brook, NJ 07058
Tel: (973) 808-9010

Lepp & Associates
www.leppphoto.com
P.O. Box 6240
Los Osos, CA 93412-6240
Tel: (805) 528-7385

Leonard Rue Enterprises
www.rue.com
138 Millbrook Road
Blairstown, NJ 07825-9534
Tel: (908) 362-6616

LumiQuest
www.lumiquest.com
28540 Durango Drive
New Braunfels, TX 78132
Tel: (830) 438-4646

Nikon, Inc.
www.nikonusa.com
1300 Walt Whitman Road
Melville, NY 11747
Tel: (631) 547-4200

Quantum Instruments, Inc.
www.qtm.com
1075 Stewart Ave.
Garden City, NY 11530
Tel: (516) 222-6000

The Saunders Group/Tiffen Company
www.saundersphoto.com
21 Jet View Dr.
Rochester, NY 14624
Tel: (716) 328-7800

Sunpak Division
www.tocad.com
Tocad America, Inc.
300 Webro Rd.
Parsippany, NJ 07054
Tel: (973) 428-9800

Vivitar Corporation
www.vivitar.com
520 Graves Ave.
Oxnand, CA 93030
Tel: (805) 988-0463s

The F. J. Westcott Company
www.fjwestcott.com
1447 Summit Street
P.O. Box 1596
Toledo, OH 43603
Tel: (419) 243-7311